Are you a
REPEAT
of Your Generation?

Are you a
REPEAT
of Your Generation?

MALESSIA J. POE

J. Kenkade
PUBLISHING®

LITTLE ROCK, ARKANSAS

Are You a Repeat of Your Generation?
Copyright © 2019 by Malessia Poe

All rights reserved. No part of this book may be photocopied, reproduced, distributed, uploaded, or transmitted in any form or by any means, or stored in a database or retrieval system, without the prior written permission of the publisher.

J. Kenkade Publishing
6104 Forbing Rd
Little Rock, AR 72209
www.jkenkadepublishing.com

J. Kenkade Publishing is a registered trademark.

Printed in the United States of America
ISBN 978-1-944486-36-5

Unless otherwise noted, scripture quotations are taken from the King James Version Bible, Public Domain.
Scripture quotations marked NIV are taken from The Holy Bible, New International Version NIV Copyright
© 1973, 1978, 1984, 2011 by Biblica, Inc. Used by permission. All rights reserved worldwide.

This book recounts actual events in the life of Malessia Poe according to the author's recollection and perspective. Some of the identifying details may have been changed to respect the privacy of those involved.

Table of Contents

My Mother's Influence on My Ministry *9*
Special Thanks *11*
Acknowledgements *13*
Introduction *15*

Chapter 1: Are you a Repeat of your Generation? *17*
Chapter 2: The Hidden Assassination *27*
Chapter 3: Sabotage *33*
Chapter 4: Coming Out of the Box of
              Confinement with Authority *41*
Chapter 5: Don't be Undermined *51*
Chapter 6: Shake the Dust off *59*
Chapter 7: Letting Go of My Past *65*
Chapter 8: Your Words Frame Your World *71*
Chapter 9: Conquering Against All Odds *83*

Letter from the Author *89*
About the Author *91*

Dedicated to my dear awesome mother,
missionary, and prayer warrior,

Jeraldean Poe Freeman

Love Forever,
Your daughter, Malessia (Lisa)

My Mother's Influence on my Ministry

I am the fourth child of seven children of the late Missionary Jeraldean Poe Freeman. My mother was my role model and allowed me to get addicted to God! God saved me in the year of 1982. My mother took me on my first missionary journey with her to witness in our hometown. She said God told her to go and take me with her. Out of the four witnessed to, three came to the Lord.

When my mom ached in her body, she would call me to come pray and God would heal my mom. My mother took me into different prisons, nursing homes, and street services with her for me to know God because she knew one day she would decrease that I may be in remembrance of all the tools and teachings she left with me that I carry on until this day. As my mother was transitioning, she reached her hand out without saying a word and shook her head up and down. She gave me her mantle. I felt the anointing; an experience I shall never forget. When my mom was ready to leave this earth, her request to me was to pray her out of here. It was one of the hardest tasks I've ever had to do, but at her request I said, "God this is my mom's will. God you said to be absent from the body is to be present with you." This book is dedicated to my dear awesome mother, missionary, and prayer warrior.

I thank God for a ministry that He has set his approval upon. I oversee higher learning for dimensional growth. In this capacity, I conduct a big back-to-school drive in a much-needed area, blessing over 500 children. I give back in the month of December to the nursing home that my mother serviced. Due to the move of God during one prison visit, the service had to be moved to the gym because the power of God was moving, and the inmates wanted to come. I have been preaching and praying for over 22 years. I am known as a prayer warrior.

Acknowledgments

In Special Loving Memory of Chief Joey

I thank God for my family, sisters, and my brothers who are very dear to me. A special thank you to my nephew, Kelly Dewayne Austin, who covered me for many years, helping me to spell the smallest of the smallest words and never giving up on me or saying "Auntie, I'm tired of you". For many years, he covered me when no one knew of my disability of not being able to spell and read while preaching and prophesying into the lives of many. I would always share with Kelly what God was saying. When God would fulfill His promise, Kelly would always say, "Auntie, I Remember." Special thanks to Kelly Dewayne Austin, Dr. Rhonda Forte, Weston Williams, and Coretta Cotton-Johnson; who took time out of their busy schedules to listen to each one of my recordings and help me that I might obey the voice of the

Lord that I heard when God said "Write this book." Even with God knowing my disability and my incapability to spell, God trusted me and put a word down on the inside of me to release to the world. I thank them for being my eyes and my ears. Thank you Coretta for being my scribe in this present time.

Thank each and every one of my family members who have believed in me down through the years. A special thanks to you my sister, Cynthia Poe Austin, Visionary for Designing Women Ministries for allowing God to use me at your Prayer Breakfast before the multitudes to showcase the glory of God.

To my godparents, Pastor Tommy and Nancy Branch who played a great part in my life by picking me up and taking me to church and to my god mom for teaching me how to spell and read and for teaching me to live by the word of the Lord that says, "After the Holy Ghost have come upon you, you shall receive power."

Love, Malessia (Lisa)

Special Thanks

Giving all honor and praise be unto He who is and is to come, My Lord and Savior, Jesus Christ who died so that I might have the awesome right of knowing my identity, to operate in the fullness and authority wherefore God has made me free. Thank God for my house of refuge known as Royal Priesthood Ministries where Apostle John Delaware serves as my Pastor and Lady Ericka Delaware as my first lady. I thank them for seeing the God in me. Thank you, Valerie Settlers for allowing God to use you to invite me to come push the power of prayer. Where would I be if it had not been for the Lord who was on my side? Through this I know I can do all things through Christ that strengthens me. I am God's child.

Much Love, Malessia (Lisa)

Introduction

The Lord God Almighty has placed it upon my heart to write this book entitled, "Are You a Repeat of Your Generation?" as an awareness to his people. God is a concerned God that wants to bring us into full development and knowledge of who we are and where we come from. It's called *identity*. Have you ever wondered where you come from?

Where it all began?

Why am I here?

As you begin to read this book, let's remove all limits, blindfolds, and denial. Let's take a walk back into time and push rewind to where it all began. God Almighty is speaking to the hearts and minds of his people, whom he loves so dearly. Ask yourself this question, "Am I a repeat of my generation?" As you read throughout this book, take inventory and discover your true identity. Ask yourself, what is my true DNA?

Life is a valuable lesson that we can all learn

from and will continue as long as we live. Some days will be good and some days will be more challenging, but through it all, God wants us to stand steadfast in the liberty wherefore he has made us free.

The key word is *free*! If we keep the consciousness of God, we can reject anything that comes our way and remain free in liberty. Grace and Mercy have set us free from the yoke that is called bondage.

One

ARE YOU A REPEAT OF YOUR GENERATION?

In the beginning when God created the heavens and the earth, everything was void. Darkness covered the face of the earth and the spirit of God moved upon the face of the deep. With God, everything existed in his mind. God spoke the radiation of his mind. It wasn't until God spoke that everything began to line up. God spoke with authority and said; **"Let there be light" and there was light.** Genesis is the beginning of where it all began. Let's go to the creation of man. The bible tells us that God created man in his image and in his likeness.

God formed man from the dust of the earth and man became a living representation. The particle, Adam was produced. God saw that it wasn't good that man be alone. God put Adam into a deep sleep. He took the rib out of Adam's side and formed wo-man. God presented the woman unto Adam. Adam named her Eve. She was created to walk by his side. She was created to produce. God gave Adam dominion and power.

It was always God's will that they should live an abundant life. It was God's will that they should never die. It was God's will that they be just as he was. God gave a commandment unto Adam, "Thou shall not eat of the tree of knowledge of good and evil." Lucifer, the third party, put the serpent on an assignment. The serpent went to the weaker vessel and convinced her to go against God, the one that created her. He sent a serpent to convince her mind to eat from the forbidden tree. *This was a setup.* After she ate, it was her job to convince her husband to eat.

> *Satan, also known as Lucifer, is already damned.*

Love will make you into a fool. Adam became blind and went against the commandment of what the creator had spoken. A penalty had to be paid for the disobedience: Adam had to work by the sweat of his brow; the woman, Eve had to bare labor pains; and the serpent had to crawl on his belly. Satan, also known as Lucifer, is already damned. As you begin to read "Are you a repeat of your generation?" I want you to know that there is life after a bad situation. It all started from the beginning.

In hearing the question, "Are you a repeat of your generation?"

I said, "God, what are you asking?"

God said, "I want you to think: are you free or are you bound? Are you walking in your grandfather's, grandmother's, father's, or mother's footprints? You see, I have given you your set of shoes and identity just as I did Adam in the beginning of Genesis. I gave him dominion and power. I put before him good and evil."

Adam became blind when he went against God and it put us all under a generational curse. Where there was no sin, Adam put us all in jeopardy.

When God put each and every one of us here on earth, it was his plan that we walk in the fullness of life wherefore he had made us free. The bible lets us know that there is nothing new under the sun. God has now given us our own consciousness to know right from wrong due to the repercussions of Adam. When Adam was created, he was created with power and authority to live forever. He knew no sin.

He knew God *one on one*.

When we were created, we were created in God's image and in the likeness of God, which is our father. When we look at ourselves, we should see the reflection of God. For when God created us, we were on God's mind. We should see purpose. We should see all that God says we are. We are walking in the divine will of God.

Am I a repeat of my generation?

As you take the time to reflect back over your generation, examine if your generation is yet positive or negative. What volume remains? Let us do an inventory check. Pause. Think about it. Ask yourself what was the most valuable thing that made my family great and what can I do to make it even greater?

> *If my mother was rejected, does that mean that the spirit was passed on to me, but was lying dormant?*

What were some of the issues?

Do they still remain until this day from my generation?

Have I been branded?

Have I been marked?

Is my generation pure or is it nasty?

If my mother was rejected, does that mean that the spirit was passed on to me, but was only lying dormant?

Am I a repeat of my generation?

Were you familiar or well-known with a preacher in the family from generation to generation to have spoken God's word but led by no example?

Was the only example do as I say, but not as I do that ended up killing the little belief that you had in God?

In prospective, we understand that every family will have their various problems and various secrets.

However, has anyone ever taken the time out to evaluate this generational cycle or curse, or was it placed in the dark room for the light not to shine on it, and it remained a family secret from generation to generation?

Am I a repeat of my generation?

As you take the time to reflect back over your generation, examine if your generation has ever dealt with things such as Alzheimer's, arthritis, high blood pressure, diabetes, cancer, mental illness, alcoholism, drug abuse, domestic violence, or gambling. Have you noticed that when you go to see any doctor for the first time, they always want to know your family history? Have you ever wondered or wanted to know why they always ask this question? It's because they feel like history always repeats itself.

When you go to doctors/physicians, you look for them to have the answer to your problem or the solution to whatever illness you are complaining about that has plagued your generation. It was a root from your family generation.

The doctor does not have the final say so, but in your mind, you're thinking, "My grandfather, grandmother, father, mother, uncle, aunt, sister, or brother died from this generational curse. Now here I am with the same diagnosis."

But I will say, why die before your time when you can live and beat all of the odds?

The family tree represents the root of where we have all come from and where it all began. Issues bring forth the root from where it all starts from. Sometimes, we are judged from our family past and their issues. We should be positive. Remember everything has a beginning and we serve notice for it to end.

Many have died knowing their family was cursed, but nobody did anything to lift the bands.

Is it true that no one had the answer, or did it just remain a blockage?

Let's go through some more links.

It has been said, history repeats itself.

A mother can tell her daughter how she is "acting just like her daddy" in a negative, high pitched voice, making a void statement.

She is only speaking a cycle of what she remembers: her mother's words from the past. Why would she damage her daughter? Because she was damaged. Her mother damaged her. **The link: the cycle repeating itself in another generation into the child's life.** This example could very well be labeled as a generational curse.

So, this is the time to really reflect and ask yourself, *Are you a repeat of your generation?*

Once you have determined your answer, define how you can move forward and break the cycle.

Coming into awareness: Awareness is simply acknowledging that you see what you see. Awareness will allow an individual to identify what has been manifested throughout their generation.

A lot of times when you are in denial, you will not accept awareness. You push reject because of rejection. You are being yet held hostage from your generation that really had nothing to do with you, but they made it about you, because of family limitations, conditions, terms, molds, and in the state of mind that they once walked in; also known as patterns and resistance. It's like sleeping in a house with rats and roaches—contaminated and condemned. Pause…inventory…checkpoint.

Let's move further into this awareness. What is a pattern? It's a guide that you have either seen or heard about. A pattern can be a brand or duplicate copy, but there is only one original. Who became the copycat? Children have seen patterns; negative and positive. What do you think stands out the most in a child's mind?

My coming into the world seemed so negative, because my mother was unmarried when she conceived and brought me forth. My daddy was married, you know a preacher, when he connected with my mother. My mom had knowledge that he was married when she produced me.

According to Isaiah 66:9, God's word says, "For I am God and I open up the womb." My birth and your birth were validated. We are here on purpose to break a generational curse. Society would call me a mistake. They would call me a bastard child.

I remember so well being mocked, "Who is your daddy?"

Something that was funny to them brought me no joy.

Many times, we look at our parents as our example. A lot of times we say, "Monkey see, monkey do," but I want to make an announcement with full effect.

According to Jeremiah 29:11; "For I know the plans that I have toward you said the Lord, plans to prosper you and not harm you, plans to give you hope and a future." If you notice the word *plans*, it has weight; it has significant meaning; and an abundance of blessing. The burn bans are on, no more spreading. We are cutting off the spread of generational curse.

In studying the genealogy of Jesus Christ, I learned and understand that our redeemer and savior came through 42 generations. Let's look at his family account.

It was polluted (negative).

It was tainted (negative).

There was much blood that was slain (negative).

There were liars (negative)...

and thieves(negative)...

His generation wasn't perfect.

His generation made mistakes (negative). But Jesus couldn't help the lineage that was chosen for him to come through.

Even though he came through a polluted generation, he came to make a difference (*positive*). That's why as I look at the number 42, I want to add them together: four plus two equals six; which represents the number of man. He was chosen, the man that came with a purpose and that purpose was to defeat, derail, and invest. He was the element to correct the imbalance and injustice that had gone through his generations. *Chosen*!

> We are here on purpose to break a generational curse.

Let's look at Psalm 51:7. It reads, "Purge me with hyssop and I shall be clean: wash me, and I shall be whiter than snow."

All have sinned. In Matthew Chapter 1, there was much need for correction. Rahab the harlot, who in today's language would be called a whore, gave birth to Boaz, who married Ruth and they birthed forth Obed, who was the father of Jesse, who was the father of David. His generation was down and needed an overhaul. They had chemistry imbalance. David was a murderer, but was known as King David, but not "The King". It was all a setup for the true King which had to come through 42 generations.

Jesus Christ's ancestors had rank in their name unto this day and we read about them through the Word of God. Jesus had to arrive on the scene to change the account from negative to positive.

After the arrival of our Lord and Savior Jesus Christ, John the Baptist tells us that no one was worthy to unlace his shoes!

He was the High Priest and the Holy One that was touched with the feelings of our infirmities.

Why did John speak of Jesus Christ's shoes? Shoes carry great weight.

Shoes travel.

Shoes can lead you into righteousness or unrighteousness. Ask yourself this question, "Where do my shoes lead me?"

Two

THE HIDDEN ASSASSINATION

Matthew 2:1 informs us that Jesus was born in Bethlehem of Judea in the days of Herod, the king. When King Herod heard that Jesus was born, he became troubled; he and all Jerusalem with him. He called them all together and demanded, "Where is he that is born King of the Jews?" They knew that a new governor would come and rule. The Assassination was against Jesus. King Herod plotted privately against this baby Jesus. An assassination was being set up against him. The wise men that were seeking Jesus to worship him were advised by King Herod, "Once you have found him, return with the information that I may come and worship him also."

It was because he needed his opponent assassinated. King Herod received more information than his mind could contain. King Herod was seeking to inflict death on Jesus. His mind became dangerous, seeking for revenge.

Assassination carries a hidden agenda. That spirit had sat upon King Herod to destroy the baby before he could live and carry out his assignment. Jesus came to give life and couldn't afford to be assassinated by King Herod. King Herod was intimidated because his reign was coming to an end. Being warned by God, the wise men returned back unto their homeland.

Assassination vs. Existence Life

King Herod was blind to think that God would allow him to kill the promised King. Assassination is a dark realm. In the month of February 2018, God began to deal with me to send forth a word unto the world that has been hiding. An assassination has always existed. This condition hit planet Earth once Satan (also known as Lucifer) was kicked out of heaven to never have a chance to return, knowing that he is damned unto damnation to be destroyed. Satan wants to take as many souls with him that he can.

Satan also knows the love that God has for all of mankind. Satan knows sin is an enemy against God. Sin is an assassin. It's a dark realm that tries to assassinate your life.

Assassination is an assault and attack and is just as violent and vicious as the master, Satan who harasses victims so his job can be carried out. In any assassination, innocent blood is shed. There is a hidden agenda against an individual's life. People have come up dead. From that day to this day, no one knows what happened. Satan works behind the scene to kill and destroy them. The assassination seeks the mind.

Let's revisit President John F. Kennedy. He and his family were riding in the motorcade. He didn't know that he was only moments away from a hidden assassination, which caused him his life. Satan is always working behind the scene to see how he can create death; to see how he can kill; to see how he can rob.

> *Sin is an assassin. It's a dark realm that tries to assassinate your life.*

Dr. Martin Luther King Jr. had no idea that when he visited Memphis, Tennessee that a hiding assassination awaited him. He was also shot. His blood was shed. Family is then left to grieve over their loved ones. It's not fair. Satan always wants to take something that he can't give and that's life.

Romans 7:21 says, "When I would do good, evil is present with me." The body that we all live in is subject to death but not assassination. I have sounded the alarm. What are we going to do about the alarm sound? Satan is sending out an assassin throughout the land to take individuals out whether it is through our home land, other countries, rebellion, or through hatred. I want to put a plea out. God wants me to inform you. All of the ones that I briefly mentioned were very great and powerful, living out their dreams and visions. Someone that's reading this book, you knew that you could have been or should have been dead, but God allowed you to escape.

> *The body that we all live in is subject to death but not assassination.*

Does it stop there? *No.* When Satan releases a demon to be assigned unto you and he doesn't carry out his duty, that demon is punished. Death had a certificate with your name on it. All praise unto God, we are yet alive!

Awareness from God

If you marry someone that's not in the will of God, that's an assassin. If you allow someone to come into your marriage and destroy it, that's an assassin. Anything that's an enemy against God is an assassin. Even that person that you thought *really* loved you; they ended up being your enemy, but all along you were making soul ties with your enemy.

People can assume that a person loves them but to their surprise, it's a cover up. Satan wants to make sure that you are seduced, bound, and blindfolded and the way he does this is by dressing everything up.

Once the mask has been taken off, you realize that Satan was playing the joker. You feel like humpty dumpty and feel like you are broken into pieces and need to be put back together again. You may look in the mirror and see a reflection of someone in your family or you may have performed some of their characteristics such as that of your mother, father, uncle, aunt or someone that was a close family friend that was always around or that you looked up to.

I want to tell you to take the mask off. Let the real you hang out. Let the real you be notified that I am not ashamed of where I came from, because I now know where I am headed.

Three

SABOTAGE

What is sabotage? It's when the enemy tries to come in and turn your world upside down and inside out. 1 Peter 5:8 states, "Be sober, be vigilant; because your adversary, the devil, as a roaring lion, walketh about, seeking whom he may devour." He is what the bible calls an accuser of the brethren. He asked God for permission to put Job on trial. Let us use our judicial court system as an example. There is one judge. There are lawyers who have agreed to take your case and stand the gap on your behalf. There are witnesses. When the case has been heard, the jury goes into deliberation to make a decision, then a judgement is rendered: guilty or not guilty. In this case, God served as all of the above against Job's accuse, who was Satan. "Now there is a day when the sons of God came to present themselves before the Lord and Satan came also among them. And the Lord said unto Satan, Whence came thou? Then Satan answered the Lord and said, from going to and from, walking up and down in it; seeking whom I may devour" (Job 1:6-7). **Sabotage!** God put a bid out on Job. God believed in Job. He was Job's witness, his lawyer, jury, and judge. Satan also was a witness. He witnessed the hand of God's protection around Job. He asked for permission from Job's attorney, who was God, to call Job into court.

> *"Be sober, be vigilant; because your adversary, the devil, as a roaring lion, walketh about, seeking whom he may devour." 1 Peter 5:8*

Guilty vs Not Guilty

His statement was, "Look at what all he has; let's make a deal: If you turn Job over into my hands, I will make Job curse you to your face."

God said, "Suffer it to be so!" Satan left with permission to sabotage Job's life.

Job was summoned into court, not knowing for what reason. One of the things that Job didn't know was that his accuser used *false accusations* against him, looking at all that Job had obtained in life and God had to prove him wrong.

LET US GO INTO COURT

God had given Satan permission to try Job which allowed Satan to summons Job into court, into his world, to sabotage him; believing Job would curse God to his face. In a matter of moments, Job's world was turned upside down.

Sabotage
  1st case: He lost his oxen.
  2nd case: He lost his sheep.
  3rd case: He lost his camels.
  4th case: He lost his children.

Satan would always allow one to escape to bring the report back to Job. He began to start losing everything. He lost his children, his house, all of his oxen, and his asses. Job began to go through a process that he was not familiar with. The bible speaks on how Job shaved his head; then, he went down to the ground and began to worship God. When you are at your lowest point, there is no time for you to throw in the towel. There is no time for you to begin to curse your life like Satan wants you to.

The best thing that you can ever do while you are going through a sabotage is to begin to worship the Almighty God, the Creator, and tell God how great he is, because number one, nothing can come to us unless God has already signed off on it.

Have you ever noticed that you have the authority in your pocket called a checkbook, but the check is no good if your name hasn't been signed? God signed off on it, knowing that he could trust Job to go through the process.

The bible says on how Job's friends came to him accusing him, wanting to know, "What have you done? We saw you blessed, but now we're looking at you being cursed." Yet, Job opened not his mouth and said a word. It's something about when things in your life and your world begin to be turned upside down and it takes you to a dark place and you begin to wonder what in the world is going on. That was the plan that Satan had for Job. God knows best.

The best thing that you can ever do while you are going through a sabotage is to begin to worship the Almighty God

When the lawyer visits the client, he assures him: "I'm the one for the job; that's why I took on the case."

I had faith in you. I had confidence, I knew that you would worship me whether you understood it or not.

WHEN GOD BECOMES YOUR WITNESS

The bible tells us that God said let me testify unto you Job: "Where were you when I put the stars in the sky? I was always here in the beginning and I shall be with you at your end."

Let's go to the conclusion of this. Everything that Job lost, everything that was sabotaged, God gave him double for his trouble.

I'll tell you through this book that it's okay to cry as long as you are crying in the presence of God and giving God the glory, to know that if he brought you to it, know that God Almighty will take you through it. *So Job's life is an example of a life being sabotaged and how God sits on his throne,* knowing that we here on earth are going to trust Him through a sabotage.

SABOTAGED IN ORDER TO BRING GOD'S NAME GLORY

A promise is a promise: Joseph's life was sabotaged by his own DNA, his brothers. They hated him, because his father favored and loved him. His father Jacob had him in his old age and made him a coat of many colors.

When God gives you a dream: God gave Joseph a dream on how the sheaves had begun to bow before him. His brothers got jealous over the coat of many colors and the dream he shared with them. They hated him and set out to kill him. They would have killed him if it had not been for Reuben. They sold him over into the hand of the Midianites, who sold him over to the Ishmaelites, who sold him to the Egyptians. Everything Joseph went through was a setup to ruin the dream, to cause the dream to die. He went through so many obstacles: he was lied on; Potiphar's wife tried to have him; he was placed in prison; he was lied to, saying he would be remembered to only be forgotten; and he was left to die not one time, not two times, but several times. Every time death was prevalent, he escaped it because the dream had not come to pass. Every test and every trial that Joseph had to go through was representative of his strength and of his power.

Joseph had to be sabotaged that he may be the one that showed favor unto his family who rejected him.

He was the one that God chose to suffer only but for a season.

The word of the Lord says weeping may endure for a night but *joy* cometh in the morning.

He couldn't die because his morning had not arrived yet. His life depended upon other ones' living. Like some of you; you may be going through and nothing is looking good. You know the devil tries to come and sabotage our minds to make us be seduced with a dark realm. Reject it. Joseph had to be sabotaged that he may be able to be the one that showed favor unto his family who rejected him.

When favor is upon your life, nothing is in motion, nothing is being manifest; it's only a dream; you can't see the vision nor provision; everything is stagnant; and nothing is moving forward, I want to prophesy and speak words of life: Remember, it's not over. The best is yet to come!

Four

COMING OUT OF THE BOX OF CONFINEMENT WITH AUTHORITY

Let us deal with coming out of the box. I am sure that we are all familiar with Christmas where people go out of their way to make sure different ones are happy and are also surprised at this particular time of year. They are guessing at what would make you/their loved ones' happier and brighten up the smile on their faces. At Christmas, people get in what they call the "Christmas Spirit" and are usually more giving and more apt to show love or what they feel like love is. Some of you; however, are saying, "Only if they knew. They don't have a clue that I'm almost unglued." Camouflaging is a disguise, hiding how you really feel and hiding all of your issues. Just like that beautifully wrapped present, you are all dressed up with your makeup on, maybe covering up a black eye or bags under your eyes from the stressors of life. You cannot allow them to see underneath the surface.

Underneath the surface, there is a caution sign that says *beware*.

Beware: I'm easy to break.
Beware: I'm at the verge of a nervous breakdown.
Beware: Tensions are raging high.
Beware. Beware. Beware.

You see the gifts wrapped so beautifully and it reminds you of who you are.

You are beautiful, but in a box.
Torn up, but in a box.

You reason in your mind to pull out the gift but wish it could stay inside of the beautifully wrapped box. Just like that gift, God wants to display the real you, but you are content with being in the box. Some people buy gifts that they take to various places so that they can have them shipped and it depends on what the box contains as to what it is marked with. For example, the label may read: fragile, handle with care, contains glass, or very easy to break. Once the box is sent off, the sender is waiting for it to arrive to its destination. The sender addresses it to who its being sent to and also includes their return address.

After they ship it, they wait patiently to receive a happy response from the person on the receiving end with the words, "I have received a package from you on today!" They hear the expression in their voice with them yet not knowing what's in the packaged box and it puts a smile on their face. As I just pointed out to you, the receiver is in expectation of what's in the box not knowing, but yet smiling. A lot of you have been placed in a box by life, and by the world; society has beaten up on you and you've been labeled with many different things. Have you ever noticed that no *one* box looks the same? They come in all different shapes, sizes, and colors, from all different places all around the world. It may not have come the same way.For example, some come by U.S. Postal, UPS, or FedEx.

You've had to deal with labels from your generation. You've had to address malice which is hatred or mistreatment.

A lot of you have been placed in a box by life, and by the world; society has beaten up on you and you've been labeled with many different things.

You've had to address someone saying, "You're just like your dad or mom."

You may have been the little girl who was mistreated and got pregnant as a teen and when you look back, you see that mom was the same age or that young boy who never really grew up, but now you are a grown man wishing you didn't have to deal with life. You look one way on the outside but there is yet something inside of the box.

Now, when you look back on the generations before you, you see that there was a seed planted inside of you that laid dormant until you reached a certain age.

Daddy got killed at a young age so you're saying, "What's the use? My hero, my idol, died young so now I'm not afraid of dying or being an alcoholic."

In your mind, you are looking and have observed your family's history and you're so sure that's how your life will be or you're looking, and you are content with where you are, because none of your family ever completed school or went to college. All you have ever known is the "ghetto life."

Let's deal with another issue that goes with the ghetto life that you have seen as a pattern in your generation. It's called "OG". That means that you are an original gangster. A lot of you are familiar with being connected to a gang or being connected to being a pusher. But as an "OG", you get in this gang because you are all familiar with the hard times of life. Being an OG/Original Gangster, all you know is Gangster. Because your daddy was an OG. So you either chose to be a blood, a crip, vice lord or whatever your gang was called, but being a gangster or in a gang you had to be initiated in. It was something you made up in your mind that you wanted to do. You looked up to your "OG". You looked up to your homies. You knew it was a life or death situation, but you blocked it all out, because of the anger and frustration of life that you've gone through and that you saw your family go through. Or you may have seen other family members who have made it as far as being an "OG" because their life was D.D.D.—Disturbed, Destructed, Destroyed. But, have you noticed that a lot of your homies are in their final resting place because they thought the negative that was in them, the anger, the frustration made them not be afraid to die. But I want to tell you on today… Don't be afraid to live! Don't be afraid to take a turning point and make life worth living.

Don't be afraid to live! Don't be afraid to take a turning point and make life worth living.

Some of you have questioned why momma had

to leave early or why daddy had to clock out/die so early, but there is yet a choice you can make to live or to die. We all have a story to tell and I come to tell you it's time for your debut. It's time for your debut in your role called "bounce back". The film has marked your life one way, but today you can say "I have my new role".

You feel like you have been marked with everything that made up your box by generational curses, labels, and things that you think you can't overcome, but I come to tell you that **you have been x'd to exit**; not touched by the labels of what people say. The film has marked your life, but today is your debut which is the act of beginning something new or to present for the first time to the public. It's time for your debut in your new role with a new direction, a new kick off, and a new introduction. So now you can say, "Roll out the red carpet for my new entrance because I have just exited out of "The Box".

God sent Jesus. He was sent, but he was also despised, rejected and mocked; but he yet had a purpose for being sent. He opened not his mouth and said not one word because he knew that he had to fulfill his purpose for being sent to the earth.

This is what I want to tell you: *Anytime you can allow the enemy to take you back into something or a behavior that happened in the past, he can only take you because you allow your mind to be opened up to something that he shows you,* but we have the power and the capability to not follow.

When I was coming up I remember going to J.C. Cook Elementary School in Arkansas. The teacher with authority would line us up to follow in a single line. We did as instructed. Now that you are of age, make wiser decisions and don't give Satan the authority to take you to a dark place that you no longer live at…the element of elementary. The bible tells us "When I was a child, I spake as a child, I understood as a child, but when I became a man I put away childish things." It will bring about an interruption where he's trying to get in between that which is going on between you and God. In other words, the reason why you're in the fight of your life is because Satan has peeped into your future. Don't allow a dark spirit to take you somewhere that God has delivered you from.

We all have a story to tell and I come to tell you it's time for your debut.

"Satan, why are you bringing it back now? Why now?" Because number one, you're walking into your ministry, you're walking into the manifestation of knowing God. Don't go ten steps backwards. Redeem the time. Be like Jonah and do a three day journey in one day. *Push* to your destiny. The only reason why Satan can lead you back to something that's dark is to ask for your permission. It's a setup. **Warning before destruction. Don't receive or sign the permission slip.** Send it back to the sender!

In Romans 8, God tells us that once you really repent, there is no condemnation to them who walk after Christ Jesus and not after the flesh. Don't let Satan bring anything from the past back. You take authority. You remind him, "I don't live there anymore!" The door has been slammed shut. I won't be weighed down from something that happened then. Nothing will disturb my walk. I walk in the newness of life. You are a product of your creator, but Satan would love for you to regurgitate. We do not walk in doubt when we believe that God has delivered us and that God has heard us. It is illegal for Satan to try to bring up your past, but it is legal to let him know:

> *"I live by the principal of God's word. I am not challenged. I am ordained. I am not ashamed of the gospel of Jesus Christ, for it is the power of God unto salvation. Every spirit is subject; you're under my feet, I walk in the authority of God. When I speak, I demand and command; the blood of Jesus is against you and you can't cross the bloodline. You will not bring my past up to me. I don't live at that address anymore! Your final notice has been served."*

Are You a REPEAT *of Your Generation?*

You don't have to be confined. If your generation was negative, that does not mean that you have to be confined to that or imprisoned by it. God said in the word that He has made a way of escape. So now my question to you is

"Do you want to come out?" Do you want to come out of whatever has had you confined and whatever has had you locked up?

When Jesus met the woman with the infirmity where it says that she was bent over, he began to decree from out of his mouth, "Woman thou art loosed."

God is not prejudiced. The word of the Lord says he came that we may have life and have it more abundantly. God said in his word that there is neither male nor female, but that we are all the sons of God. God is saying to tell you; you may have had a slave mentality, but God wants to bring you out of bondage into this marvelous light. Somebody might say, well it's looking dim for me, but it's like when you're driving a car and is gets dark late over in the midnight hour and you can hardly see. You are on the road or path that you've never driven or gone down before. You hit the switch and turn the light on high beam. **God is saying to you, "I am that beacon of light that sit upon a hill that cannot be hidden."** So God is saying to tell his people, "You do not have to be confined."

Come out! Come out with your hands up! Even a police officer tells you upon pulling you over and arresting you to "Lift your hands!" That means you're saying, "God I surrender." You surrender to the one that carries the authority. Because you see him dressed in the police uniform, you respect him. There is no greater God than we have. He sent his son Jesus that we might have a right to the tree of life, so God doesn't want us to be confined. The bible says that we can decree a thing here on the earth. The latter days shall be greater than the former.

Five

DON'T BE UNDERMINED

You don't allow the mind to speak to you. You speak to the mind. The mind carries waves. It carries brain cells. The mind is very important. It's a connection. It's so powerful that if you allow it to, it will undermine you. It is storage. It stores data from your past, your present, but allows it to speak positive to your future. It gathers information. The mind memorizes. It's a resource of things that you have gone through that's called process. The mind can be overpowering. Yes, we have to have the mind to function, but we cannot allow the mind to overpower us, overrule us, and make us think things that God has not thought concerning us. The mind can be hallucinated. The mind can go into shock; the mind can go ahead of time. Scripture says, "Let this mind be in you which is also in Christ Jesus."

Jesus' mind builds up. Jesus' mind performs miracles, and Jesus' mind had a great connection with the father. Jesus mind had a great communication with the will of God. So, don't allow your mind to be stagnated.

Let's go to the scripture in Luke 8:43-48, where Jesus saw a woman bent over from her infirmity. Her mind told her that this condition can't be fixed, but Jesus (being connected to God) saw the woman and his mind spoke to her mind and his words took effect and rebuked the defect in her mind as he said, "Woman thou art loosed." Her mind heard and she was made whole. *What is your mind hearing?*

Being in a dark place in your life can make a person miserable, unhappy, depressed, and oppressed. Being in a dark place in your life can bring major challenges for a person that already carries a defect.

What happens when you remember how you were overlooked, how you were ignored, how people laughed at you? People said, "You're just plain old sorry." They spoke violent words and you said life isn't fair because they put you in a box. Because they belittled you. Because they couldn't validate you. It was a setup for a pitfall. Sometimes in life, people will belittle you to make themselves feel good to be powerful, because of the control and authority that you gave them over your mind. Notice that I said *your* mind.

Somebody reading this book, you've been raped and I'm sorry that you had to go through that. Some of you were let down when your daddy said I'm coming to see you only to never show up or Mom ran off and left you and unto this day, it remains for you to know the true story of who you are. Don't let your DNA make you hostage because of a hard life, because of family issues, or because of the family tree. Some of you are dealing with mental illness, bipolar, schizophrenia, or anxiety. You're wondering, "Why me? Why am I down such a long, dark, cloudy road? Again, ask yourself when will I be able to breathe?" Or have you allowed gravity to suck all the life out of you? Are you reaping images that you never knew but knowing they came from somewhere, but no one will help you; no one will give you the answers? You may be wondering, "What am I supposed to do? Who am I? Am I a repeat of my generation?" Maybe you're feeling like Alice in Wonderland. May I encourage you to believe you can fly and you can touch the sky? If God's eyes are on the sparrow, I know of a surety he will take care of you. I

> *Satan took some of you that are reading this book up to the edge of the cliff, but you didn't jump.*

may not know you, but I do know with all of life's obstacles of darkness that have hovered over you, that you beat the odds, because of what you just read. You beat the odds of darkness, destruction, and death.

Satan had a job to do and he knows when one is supposed to be powerful. I am so glad you didn't flatline. You beat the odds. Satan took some of you that are reading this book up to the edge of the cliff, but you didn't jump. Grace and mercy have been allotted unto you because Satan had a case against you to make you lesser than less and more sorrowful than sorrowful. You were served unjustness, but today, we discharge all the heavy weights of darkness.

Like a tree that is planted, it doesn't know how strong it is until a storm, tornado, earthquake, or wind comes through to let it know how powerful it is. In life, it will bring all of things that I just named: tornadoes, storms, earthquakes and volcanoes to only let you know how strong you are. You can make it. You can take it. The choice is yours. The ball is in your hands. You may have wondered, "Why were my dad and mom so sorry? They had nothing to pour into me." I remember asking myself, "Why am I here?" My dad was married, but he and my mom produced two powerful women of God in the earthly realm and we are here living out our purpose. *Stop right now and pause* and thank God that they were the vehicle to get you here. Ask God Almighty to help you to walk in the spirit of forgiveness. Forgive the person that hurt you. Forgive the person that raped you. Forgive the person that belittled you. Forgive the person that kept your mind hostage to make themselves feel powerful.

Forgiveness is a powerful tool. Once you forgive, anger has got to go; hatred has got to go. We're going to bury our case on today and walk in the newness of life and we will have a positive thought instead of negative thoughts and say, "I am living proof that I beat all of the odds!"

Are you willing to change your generation through the power of prayer?

Being teased, but yet persevering; being barren, but yet believing God—this describes who Hannah was. Hannah made her way to the temple to make her request known unto God. She prayed so much until she prayed out of herself; she prayed so much that when they came into the temple, they thought she was drunk. Are you willing to change your generation through the power of prayer?

You can hit a realm in God through pushing the power of prayer. Hannah was very willing to go through birthing forth what she desired through prayer. Prayer will change any situation in your life. She was being mimicked; yet, kept praying. She was barren; yet, kept praying. Hannah knew that God brought Israel out of Egypt with an outstretched hand. A word will always spread and will always go forth whether negative or positive. Hannah made known her desire. Did it happen? Yes, it did.

Israel was afflicted by reason of their taskmaster. They were willing to yet make a cry unto God. They knew that if there was any way they were going to come out, it was going to have to be through the crying out by reason of their afflictions unto God Almighty.

> *By birthing things through,*
> *that's how you come to know*
> *God.*

So, Hannah began to say, "Let me make my way to the altar. What I need from God, I'm going to express it." Catch those words: "Express It." Hannah said, "That I may bring forth the manifestation, expressing what I want through prayer that it may be magnified to bring God's glory.

Matthew 7:7 tells us to ask and it shall be given, seek and ye shall find, knock and the door shall be open.

We have to have some Sanballats and Tobiahs that will provoke us into the presence of God. When the police come and arrest somebody on the scene, the first thing they tell them is "You have the right to remain silent." Hannah was in the temple talking to God, but no words were coming out.

She said, "In other words, God I want to keep this thing secret between me and you."

When they came and picked up on it they thought she was drunk, but she said, "I'm going to keep it silent until God steps in and shows them that he is God and that he shall impregnate me." It's good when you get the facts of the results of what things are not supposed to be. That way God can show forth his great and awesome power. Hannah said, "If I can just get to the temple, I know God is going to meet me there. God's going to know if you will stand the testing of time. By birthing things through, that's how you come to know God.

If I were in the house, had this meat to get to the smokehouse, and saw all these vicious dogs, I would be going to get me some weapons. The weapon now is the word of God. The prescription now is the word of God. So I may notice that I have vicious animals out here – women (vicious), men (vicious), employees (vicious), children not acting right – but they've got to provoke me into the presence. I'm looking at the temperature of every dog, and they are wanting what I have, but I have an assignment to get from here to the smokehouse within the next five minutes. Saying "y'all move" is not going to get it. Saying "y'all get out of the way" is not going to get it, but when you know how to participate in spiritual warfare, that's what's going to get it in this hour.

That's why the Bible says in Ephesians 6:11, "Put on the whole armor of God that ye may be able to withstand the wiles of the devil. For we wrestle not against flesh and blood, but against principalities and powers".

Do you have on your garments? You are in the fight of your life.

Have you taken a stand?

What do you do when your faith is pushed to the limit? You keep on pushing.

There was a widow who kept going before an unjust judge, saying, "Avenge me of my adversary". Remember that we have a just God.

Six

SHAKE THE DUST OFF

Shake the dust off while walking through a storm. When a windstorm comes, it can block you from seeing your view. Dust is everywhere, all over the body, but you don't just stand there. Your hand becomes a windshield blade. You can barely see, but you keep on walking. The hope is pushing through your mind. Can't see? Keep walking. The dust becomes greater as you walk. You become determined to keep pushing – crawling, yet pushing. You feel like if you drop to the ground, the dust won't be as heavy, only to realize it is even heavier. You're down from where it accumulated, so you tell yourself, "Get back up! Push! Walk! Make it! You can make it!" You no longer have to manage the dead weight or dead circumstances. I want you to manage, command, and direct your future.

Notice in this scenario that you've been up fighting, but the dust storm has knocked you down very low, and you've gotten back up dirty and dusty. Minutes seem like hours that you have been exposed to the dust from which we were accumulated. In the book of 1 Corinthians, Paul writes, "Therefore let him that thinks he stands take heed lest he fall."

Proverbs 24:16 says, "For a just man falleth seven times and riseth up again". Rise up! "Seven" is symbolic for completion. Rise up! Get your cymbals, make it to the shower, and cleanse yourself! Purge yourself with soap and be renewed with cleanness! The dust storm is over. Now that you look back, the storm has only become a day (or year) to remember. You did it. We did it. We made it across the desert storm. We made it through the trial of things not looking so good.

I proclaim the liberty. Yes, I have now *dusted the dust* and it remains to serve as my testimony. I made it. Ashes to ashes. Dust to dust. Today I chose to thrust and no longer live in the husk. In the bible, the prodigal son makes a bad decision, which results in him eating with the swine. Yet when he comes unto himself, he remembers from where he came, and his father is waiting. Satan had set him up to believe that he could make it on his own. He has spent all he had. As long as he had money, he had friends. His desire became a disaster, but one day he comes to himself and begins to remember someone: *Daddy*.

I'm sure he's embarrassed, wondering, *will Daddy receive me again?* He fights the negative thoughts in his mind. He makes up his mind, thinking, *if I can just make it back to daddy's house, I will ask him to just hire me as one of his servants*. Daddy is waiting patiently because in his heart he has always known that his son would return home. I'm sure when he meets his son, the boy has the smell of the swine on him, but there's something about a father's love. He embraces his son and is glad that he survived the desert storm.

He is just like our "Daddy", God, whose arms are open wide.

My "now" situation is *not* my end result. I am making a change right now to pick my feet up off the ground. As documented in Joel 2:28, God declares that He will "pour out [His] Spirit upon all flesh" and "[our] sons and daughters shall prophesy". Shake the dust off. David said, "Oh, taste and see that the Lord is good and His mercy is everlasting. Blessed is the man that trusts in Him". I made it because of the mercies of God. In any storm I face in life, my proclamation is: "I shall keep on believing that this too shall pass".

Now that I made it through the shaking – through the shackles – from the dust of the earth,

I am ready to face the deepest waters. Peter, in seeing Jesus walk on water, said, "Lord, if it be you, bid me to come." Even though the water looked troubled to Peter, at Jesus' word, Peter's faith caused him to step out. Peter walked on the water. I want to encourage you to never settle for where you are when there is always room for improvement. The ocean has a way of moving you from the surface into the current of the waves, often without warning. When the waves come, be in a place to *embrace* them. Step into new territory. God will not only allow the dust to settle but also command the water to back up.

God said, "Before you call me, I have already answered". What's His name? JESUS. Now step out into the deep.

Moses has died. Joshua is next in line to lead God's people into their promise. God has to assure Joshua, "Just as I was with Moses, so shall I be with thee". God gave a commandment unto Joshua, saying, "I want you to get the priest that bears the Ark of the Covenant". That was a commandment from God. God will always stick by His word. There was a river being overrun. It was called the "muddy Jordan", but the Bible details that Joshua obeyed God. As soon as the priest stepped into the Jordan River, everything became still. Something similar may manifest in your life or you may be able to relate in that sometimes it feels like you are drowning and all you can see is mud everywhere. I want to remind you that when you walk in the mud, you make footprints that will serve as a reminder of when you gave God glory and honor by obeying and praising Him. Don't wait until the battle is over. Right there, give God praise. Remember that God is Jehovah Jireh, Jehovah Nissi, Jehovah Rapha, Jehovah Shalom. God said, "Before you call me, I have already answered". What's His name? JESUS. Now step out into the deep. God just wants us to know that when trouble comes, we are supposed to cry out, "Abba!", just like Israel cried out to our Father.

God will deliver every time.

Shake the dust off.

Shake the residue off.

Shake the plagues off.

Shake the lack off.

Shake the disappointments off.

Now walk in the increased purification, blessings, and more-than-enough success. You are His troop, so keep marching on in the dust and let it be trampled under your feet. God is our General, and we are His troop. We have come up through great trials and tribulations, washing our robes in the blood of the Lamb.

Seven

LETTING GO OF MY PAST

Right now, I'm calling you into awareness of who you are. I want to serve a notice to you that a lot of things you have dealt with were in your bloodline, but it's crucial to get to know who you are! I have met people who were beautiful yet *felt* ugly. They were powerful yet *felt* powerless. They were lost and not wanting to be found, seeking attention at their lowest. They were living in stigma but didn't know their value. They were being complimented but also constantly belittled. Who beat you down? Who kicked you around? Who didn't validate you? Who shamed you? Who called you out of your name? Who didn't give you any attention?

When you feel all alone, isolated in the prison in your own mind and not knowing how to deal with harsh realization, you begin to feel like a genie in a bottle or jack-in-the-box. Out of all that you've been through, you get hit with more and more. Domestic abuse. Seduction. You're like a remote control.

Samson was a man of strength. He was a man of power. When he was born, it was with purpose. The angel of the Lord appeared unto his mother instructed her that no razor was to come upon his head because that's where his strength would reside. He was born knowing the secret was within his hair, but he got connected to a dark realm by way of a seductress named Delilah, who pretended to love him.

Have you ever been in a pretend relationship and all the devil wanted was your strength and blind love? Has anyone ever made you out to look like a fool and all you were left with was your heart in your hands? In these scenarios, you get wounded, and they're saying, "Next". All Delilah wanted was to discover the source of Samson's strength, so she could become fully equipped with the only weapon that would defeat a promised seed.

She showed the truth of who she was, but he was blind.

She announced, "Samson, the Philistines be upon you." He slayed them. The more and more engaged you become, the *weaker* you become, being sifted and losing strength, drawn in deeper.

Samson became so entangled that when he looked up, the secret was out. His hair was cut. He was no longer mighty, but weak, and unable to fight, all because he was seduced.

When you have had an issue in your life, who have you taken it to? Faith has to kick in. When Samson realized he had neither love nor hope, he was completely hopeless. God will give hope to the hopeless. You have to realize that you have an issue and ask yourself where (or to whom) you are taking your issues. For example, the woman referenced in Matthew 9:20-22, Mark 5:25-34, and Luke 8:43-48 had the issue of blood and had already taken her issues to the doctor. Someone may be dealing with an issue like malice, addiction, rape, or hatred.

However, we need to remember that we *all* have a story to tell.

We can go tit-for-tat with what problems we have, but our problems will never be solved until we make up our minds that these things embedded in us from our respective generations (generational curses), perhaps, that have run in family lines possibly deemed corrupt – can be overcome. I want to give you a promise today that you can live! You can live! Right now, tell yourself, "I can live! I am going to live on top of the mountain. I may be coming from the bottom, and the bottom may have burst out, but I am still standing".

I want to tell somebody to *push* your way back to the top.

This book was designed for God to let you know that you may not have any control over where you've been or maybe you've had some control, but because it was in your family DNA, you began to speak things into being. For example, your family may have gambled when you were a child. Now you might find yourself saying things like, " I remember that I used to gamble as a child because that's all my mom and dad ever did", but I can tell you today that if you want to come out of that pattern, you can ask God to help you come out. Tell God, "Lord, I surrender this generational curse to you. God, I realize that I have faced this problem along with my family, but today is the day that every chain shall be broken."

> *Tell God, "Lord, I surrender this generational curse to you. God, I realize that I have faced this problem along with my family, but today is the day that every chain shall be broken."*

The Bible says that God will give you power to tread upon serpents. Jesus asks, "When did the Spirit enter in?" and follows that with the answer: "As a child". As a child, many things may have happened to you because mom and dad were not there to protect you, and it left you exposed and vulnerable. It made you submit to the will of Satan, whose domain is the Realm of Darkness.

I have always pondered as to why it is so easy to turn to the spirit of darkness when Jesus said that He came so that we may have life and have it more abundantly. Some of you, having come from all across the world, may not have ever heard that, but I come to speak directly to your DNA today to be *cleaned up* in the name of Jesus.

You know, in our society, we have different programs like AA (Alcoholics Anonymous), NA (Narcotics Anonymous), and GA (Gamblers Anonymous). I come to tell you today to gird up your mind and tell yourself, "I am coming out and looking to you Lord". My experience is that I used to be strung out on drugs, smoking cigarettes, and drinking at a young age, but I'm so glad I made Jesus my choice. I kicked the habit.

Eight

YOUR WORDS FRAME YOUR WORLD

I am sure that in life we have all heard these statements: "I'm down to my last dime", "I don't know how", "I don't have enough money for this", or " I hit rock bottom". Let's deal with "rock bottom". When you hit rock bottom, there is nothing for you to do but swim or climb up until you break the surface. You have to remain positive and think, *I may be at the bottom, but I'm going to make my way back up to the top*. Jesus' words are very powerful, and they hold up to this day. In John 2:19, He says, "Destroy this temple, and in three days I will raise it up again." When the veil was torn, it allowed us access to the inner court of God and made it possible to speak with Him directly. What happens when you hear yourself speak? It *should* activate your faith. Faith comes by hearing and hearing by the word of God. Jesus spoke with authority – "Destroy this temple, and in three days I will raise it up again". I'm going to show you that your words have reverberating power. You will see the resurrection power of your own words, just as Jesus did.

The proclamation was given to His disciples. There are many times in life when seeing is believing. I'm sure the disciples went on with their daily duties yet moaned that Jesus was no longer in their presence. I'm sure they were thinking, *He told us he wasn't going to be with us long, but He showed us great signs and wonders!* Mary went to the tomb to anoint Jesus' body, and an angel stood at the gate of the tomb. The angel had a message. How many of you know that much of what happens in the Bible lines up with what has already been spoken?

The Bible says that when they went into the tomb of Jesus, He had folded the sheet that was over Him and laid it there very neatly, as if to say, "I'm leaving this as a sign that I have risen". The angel of the Lord came with a message, saying, "Why seek ye the living among the dead? He is risen. Remember that he had decreed it". Jesus' words resonate throughout his execution and subsequent resurrection: "Destroy this temple, but in three days I'm going to raise it up again".

We've got to know that we have the power of life and death in our tongues, and whatever we speak has the power to manifest in alignment with the universe.

I'm telling you that you can speak at top volume! Speak: "I might be at the bottom, but I'm coming up! I'm coming up on the rough side, but I'm coming up! I've *got* to come up!" Your words are framing your world.

The Bible says that, upon His resurrection, Jesus went to Hell, took the keys, and gave them to us. Keys represent *authority*. When you know you have authority, you don't have to break into your own house. All you have to do is use your keys. Use your keys of authority. Use your "hind's feet", your power, to trample upon serpents, in the name of Jesus. Through this book, I command that you rise up! You might be at the bottom, but all you have to do is lift up your eyes to the hills from where your help comes. If you don't mind, take a moment right now, activate your faith, and say, "*All!* All of my help comes from the Lord". You may be at the bottom, but can I give you a little revelation knowledge? At the bottom means that your feet are either in troubled water or in the mud, but there isn't anything wrong with your feet. Take your liberty and put one foot in front of the other. Do a left-right-left rotation like they do in the Army. While you are on the bottom, trample and dance before God. Give God something to work with. Tell yourself, "I'm coming out of Lo-debar in the name of Jesus". Tell the devil, "I've been down long enough, but I'm on my way up! I have a new mind and new spirit".

Do you believe in yourself the way God Almighty believes in you? You were created to create.

To be on rock bottom means that you are still alive. You're standing on some kind of surface. Elevate yourself. Sometimes people say, "I've hit rock bottom – there ain't no hope", but there is hope for the hopeless. There is peace for your weariness. Don't live in the DNA that previous generations have suffered through. How can you tell someone not to live in something when they're already 21, 25, 35, 40, or even 50 years old? I come to tell you that we all can frame our minds with our words.

Don't accept the negative when there is a positive waiting for you to knock on its door and say, "What do you have to offer me?" I come to offer you life and inspiration. So you say; "I hit rock bottom". No. I want you to change your words and say; "I am headed toward the top, I am chosen, I am a favorite customer of God, I am looking for the unexpected, I am going to enjoy the rest of my life. What was, will be no more, and I am talking about while the breath (The Ruah of God) is yet in my body, because when God created me, He created me with himself in mind."

My "now" situation is not my end result. I am making a choice right now to pick my feet up off the ground.

Don't allow the mind to hold onto the wounds, scars, hurt, and pain. Time will heal, and, if you will believe and receive, it can be now. Renew your mind and renew your strength. Tell your mind to come in order. Orchestrate your mind. Bring it into harmony. Now push reset, and then rewind. You've got a mind made up to strive and reach the stars. Say no to past issues and embrace this new amazing grace.

Let us resolve to see new results. Let us rebuild again. Let us plant new soil. Let us replace old, dead, and negative and replenish with fresh fertilizer. Let us break new ground, plant new seeds, and re-harvest.

Do you believe in yourself the way God Almighty believes in you? You were created to create. Habakkuk 2:2 (NIV) states, "…Write the vision; make it plain upon tablets, so he may run that reads it". The handwriting is in this book. God is validating you all over again. Now you can write. Catch this vision and begin to write new goals. Notice I said, "rebuild". Nehemiah Chapter 4 details that Nehemiah remembered Jerusalem in its former days and how Jerusalem was destroyed, but Nehemiah worshipped God and got a letter to go and rebuild Jerusalem all over again. Did he have distractions? Yes, he did. He had Sanballat and Tobiah. However, Nehemiah made up his mind that he had a work to do and God chose him to do it. In Nehemiah 6:3, Nehemiah makes this statement to his enemies: "I am doing a great work, and I cannot come down".

There will be people who ask you, "You waited this long?" They may say something like "oh, please" or "you're setting yourself up for failure again", but I want to tell you to ignore the negative and remember what God has said about you. Everything you have gone through has been a side effect. These are just obstacles or blockades.

Remember what I said earlier in the book: Don't flatline. Prevent hindrance. Sometimes a doctor will prescribe something for you to take that he's not familiar with and doesn't know for sure will really work for you, but he prescribes it, anyway. You may not know it, but your mind tells you it's okay to take it. When you go to the pharmacist to pick up medication, they always supply a printout of all the potential side effects. Does that stop you from taking the medication? No, it doesn't because all you have in your mind is, *I need help. I need the pain to cease. I need my body to be more "at ease"*. I have a better prescription for you this day. It can be called the Word of Life, the Ruah of God, or the very *breath* of God. It's how God breathed into us and we became living souls. Every time you inhale and exhale, you are living on the oxygen of God.

Haggai 2:9 (NIV) says, "'The glory of this present house will be greater than the glory of the former house,' says the Lord Almighty. And in this place I will grant peace,' declares the Lord Almighty". Everything that you've gone through is in the past tense, and I want to let you know that God is a high priest who is touched by our infirmities and feelings – every issue, every pain, every form of demolition that you have gone through. God cares. Who cares? God cares. The Bible says, " If God is for us, who can be against us?", which stands as a reminder that the Lord, from this day forward, will fight for you.

Make a connection with God. If you plug something into a wall, you can't *see* the watts, amps, and volts behind the protective covering. That's the way it is – there is a secret place behind the wall, like the one referenced in Psalm 91, the secret place of God. So any and every time you need God, remember that you're already plugged into Him. Just activate your faith. Activate your mind and walk with your head up high, knowing that you are powerful. You are changed. You are full of *dunamis*.

Now considering all that God has said, ask yourself, "Am I a repeat of my generation?"

If your generation or bloodline brought you negativity, this book stands to give you a different outlook on life.

Notice that there are four seasons: spring, summer, fall, and winter. They don't all come at one time. Each has its own time to come forth. I want to tell you that this is your season to come forth. Spring forth like the spring.

*Your words can either
veto or release.*

You may have fallen down, but Psalm 145:14 (NIV) says, "He upholds all who fall." Summer is hot and lifts up all who are bowed down. Winter brings snow. Morning by morning, new mercies we see. So just know God is faithful. He's faithful right now. In the book of Lamentations Chapter 3 (NIV), it says, "[Your compassions] are new every morning; great is your faithfulness".

Decree this:

Life has been hard and seemed unfair, but I am no longer poor and destitute. I am now set in forward motion. I am now changing from the worst condition to another state of mind, which is founded on strength and renewal. I shall have whatsoever I say, given that the power of life and death lies within my tongue.

Take authority and remember the word "veto". I hope that you are ready to be evoked. Your words can either *veto* or *release*. In the book of Matthew, chapter 4, it says that Satan knows when to come your way. He's waiting until you're at your lowest point in life, just like he did with Jesus when Jesus got weak from fasting and became hungry. Satan came to Him and tried to tempt Him at the weakest point in His life. Jesus used the authority from His mouth, which was the word of God.

You have words inside you that could unlock the mystery of your life.

From this day forward, veto anything that comes your way and will not be conducive to where you are headed. Some of you may have been faced with challenges like life-threatening illness or strife, but I want you to take authority and say, "I veto!" Normally, for a national bill to pass, there has to be a consensus from government legislature, but the person in authority – for example, the president of the United States – can veto it at any given point, and it will have to go back to Congress, where it will then be rewritten to his or her satisfaction.

I'm here to tell you to rewrite the script of your life and remember *you* are the one standing in power. You have the power to veto anything that is not conducive to your personal walk from this day forward. Rise up out of the ashes because you are built for greatness. **I also want to tell you not to give out unless you're giving out *praise*.**

Don't you dare allow a roadblock to get in your way. Take a deep breath because I know life may be hard. Now inhale and exhale the power of God. That alone should have given you a reason to live and fight on. My sister or brother – fight on. Right there, you should have gained strength and power that is called the *"Ruah" or breath of the Almighty God.*

I want to encourage you not to be embarrassed of where you came from. We all have stories to tell. Your words can help somebody else avoid walking down the path that you and your family may have gone down.

Your life can help somebody else see the bigger picture because there may be doors you've been able to close that they still need to close. Your life can help somebody out. When everything gets dark, you may wonder how because you don't want anybody to walk in your footsteps through something that has led you to nothing but destruction. **Open your mouth and declare, "I *can* help somebody."**

Nine

CONQUERING AGAINST ALL ODDS

Romans 8:37 states, "Nay, in all these things we are more than conquerors through Him that loved us." I pray that this book has empowered you, that you have gained knowledge, that you feel like you can strive, that you feel like you have a better understanding of some of the things that you have gone through in life, and that scales have fallen from your eyes. I want you to remember that we were designed to conquer. Now that we have knowledge and awareness, we can denounce anything that tries to sink us under its weight and drown us. Let us all take the puzzle apart and start afresh by first renewing our minds. We will curse every generational curse. I refuse to be a repeat of my generation. 2

Corinthians 4:9 says, "…persecuted, but not forsaken; cast down, but not destroyed".

Most of us are familiar with the setup for a wrestling match – two opponents facing off and the object being to defeat and knock each other out. I remember preaching a sermon some years ago titled "Knocked Down, but not Knocked Out". As long as you have wind, The Ruah of God's breath in your body, you can get up and shake yourself off. You might have had some blows in life, times when the devil thought he knocked you down and out. **However, if the referee has not yet counted all the way to three, you have time to bounce back up.** Shake yourself, get back in the ring, and start all over again. Pick up where you left off. Some of you may have been in the fight of your life, but it's now time to bounce back.

Have you noticed when you throw a ball on the wall or on the ground, it comes back? Generations come back to curse us, generational curses come back to haunt us, but the Word of the Lord gives us hope. The God of Love chases after us.

Will the real survivor please stand up and run the race that is now set before you? You are a winner! I leave you with my personal testimony. The world labeled me as being illiterate. I graduated with a 1.06 Grade Point Average. However, you and I can do all things through Christ which strengthens us. I beat the odds. Philippians 2:5

says, "Let this mind be in you, which was also in Christ Jesus". **Pick up your cross and bear it.**

We are developed *to* develop. We may have been in the dark room until God finished changing our identities. Even Jesus Christ came low. He came meek and humble. He came with purpose. He knew his purpose. He strived, He persevered, and He gave it His all even in the Garden of Gethsemane. He wrestled with his decisions, but he accepted the will of His Father, who knew what was best for Him. Don't you know that God knows what is best for you?

Will the real survivor please stand up and run the race that is now set before you?

This book is designed to pick you up out of the muck and miry clay, for you to see yourself the way God sees you, for you to say that you are above and not beneath, and for you to believe that you are the lender and not the borrower.

Ask yourself what God says about you. What He says validates you, strengthens you, makes you more than a conqueror, and makes you triumphant because the Lord our God is triumphant. He has made us to be triumphant and to persevere into the greater call that He has for us.

Say bye-bye to a generational curse. Yes, you have the keys to bind and loose. You have the keys to build yourself up. You have the keys to stir up the gifts of God that are down inside you. You have the keys to tap into the mind of God. YOU HAVE THE KEYS, but are you willing to use the authority God has given you by handing you the keys? Now we can go into the inner courts, into the mind of God, and seek Him. I don't care how low you might be; God is able to pick you up, dust you off, and put you back in the race. Run the race that is set before you and endure your cross of suffering. Your cross might have brought you some shame. Dust yourself off, decree and declare whether it's been negativity or ups and downs in life, but boldly determine that you will not be a repeat of the negativity that was rooted in your generation.

> *Ask yourself what God says about you. What He says validates you, strengthens you, and makes you more than a conqueror*

For the Word of the Lord says, "…you shall be like a tree that is planted by the rivers of water". If you notice a tree's design, it has roots that go deep into the earth, so that when storms come, the tree is so embedded in the earth that nothing can uproot it and nothing can pluck it up. We have to see ourselves as being like that tree that stands against all odds that come against it.

Knowing that, we can inhale and exhale. Knowing that, we shall be, we shall be, we shall be! We shall be greater than great and more than more. **Then, we will put out the energy of who God says we are.** I will not live in a dark place, for where there is *darkness* there is *lowliness*. Where there is darkness, all the attributes of the dark realm appear. God has called us to walk into His marvelous light, where we don't have to be entangled with a yoke of bondage. What is a yoke of bondage? It's when Satan has you in his clutches, in his handcuffs, and he has decreed a death sentence on you, but God has decreed *life and life more abundantly.*

Know this: You *don't* have to be a repeat of your generation. You don't have to walk through the trail where the popcorn was left for you to find your way. God said, "For I am the light of the world. A city that sits on a hill cannot be hidden". **Don't walk in the negativity of your generation.**

You may say, "I don't have anybody", "I am lost", or "I don't know my family identity". Let me give you awareness that God wants to write you into His Will and create you to be who He says you are. Drop the baggage, pick up God, and strive to be better than what you used to be. See God as greater than any problem. See God as greater than your situation. Isaiah 40:31 says, "For we shall run and not be weary, we shall walk and not faint". Know that you are walking with the best source, which is God Almighty, your best connection. You plug a light into a wall looking for it to produce the power that you need for the appointed time. *Catch it by the spirit.* Being plugged into God gives us the capability to *produce* power. Walk in victory throughout the rest of your days!

Letter from the Author

My own life was sabotaged in writing this book....

In the month of July, the 26th day of 2018, there was a crash that came to destroy my life to keep me from getting this word out. In the month of September of this year, the spirit of the Lord came with a prophetic word: "I have given you a cloak." God showed me three days before the wreck a dream of me being in a car wreck, but I would survive it. The impact was so hard that they heard it way up on the 13th floor. My nephew made an echo into the heavens. If I had to describe it, it was like a *shabaq*. They called the wreck a trauma wreck. It was sent to take us out of here, but God blocked it. Satan knew that this book was ordained by God, until he sent forth a dark realm to collide here on earth, but God had already signed off on it.

Let's speak naturally that you may understand the spiritual. Let's deal with the stock market; we wait on the report of the market. There have been reported times when the stock market crashed, but you waited patiently for it to come back up. What you thought you lost you only gained. I lost my memory for three days, but God restored it. I gained more by enduring the hardship as a good soldier in the Army of the Lord. I was made for this battle. Sabotage, you lost. God, you won and get all of the Glory. I beat the odds. I pray that through this book that the knowledge that God has blessed me to be able to share with everyone who reads it has blessed you. If this book has been a blessing to you, I would love to hear from you.

You can email me at malessiapoe@yahoo.com
You may also go to my webpage at malessiapoe62.wixsite.com/lisapoe.

May the peace of God rest upon each and every one of you.

Sincerely Yours,
Malessia J. Poe, Author

About the Author

MALESSIA J. POE

Photography credit: J. Kenkade Publishing

Malessia oversees a higher learning program for dimensional growth whereby she conducts a big back to school drive in underprivileged areas blessing over 500 children each year. She's an avid volunteer each December at the nursing home where her mom serviced. Maleissa is an ordained minister and has been preaching and praying for over 22 years. She is affectionately known by others as a prayer warrior.

J. Kenkade
PUBLISHING®

Publish Your Book With Us

Our All-Inclusive Publishing Package
Professional Proofreading & Editing
Interior Design & Cover Design
Manuscript Writing Assistance
Competitive Pricing & More

For Manuscript Submission or other inquiries:
jkenkadepublishing.com/manuscript-submissions
(501) 482-JKEN

J. Kenkade
PUBLISHING®

Hire A Ghostwriter!

Your Voice. Our Pen.

We'll Write Your Book For You
You're Still the Author
Payment Plans Available
All Ghostwriters are Degreed and Experienced

For Ghostwriting inquiries:
jkenkadepublishing.com/ghostwriting
(501) 482-JKEN

Also Available from J. Kenkade Publishing

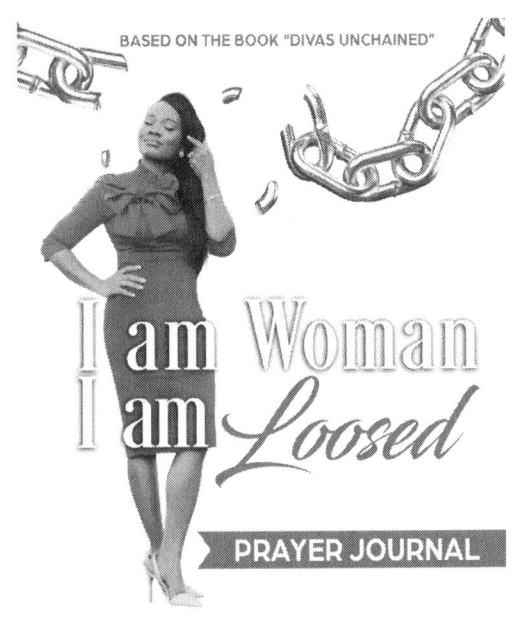

I am Woman I am Loosed — PRAYER JOURNAL
BASED ON THE BOOK "DIVAS UNCHAINED"

DR. NIOKA SMITH

ISBN: 978-1-944486-38-9
Purchase at jkenkadepublishing.com or drniokasmith.com

Having trouble getting through the day? Stuck in one or more areas of your life that you can't seem to shake? Feeling like the weight of the world is on your shoulders? Feeling stagnant or cheated out of things in life? Use this prayer journal to help guide you in praying your way through as you work on breaking free and/or staying free. Declare that you will no longer be controlled by life circumstances. Experience the uncompromising truth through powerful affirmations provided by the author and very applicable bible verses that leads to spiritual and emotional transformation.

Also Available from J. Kenkade Publishing

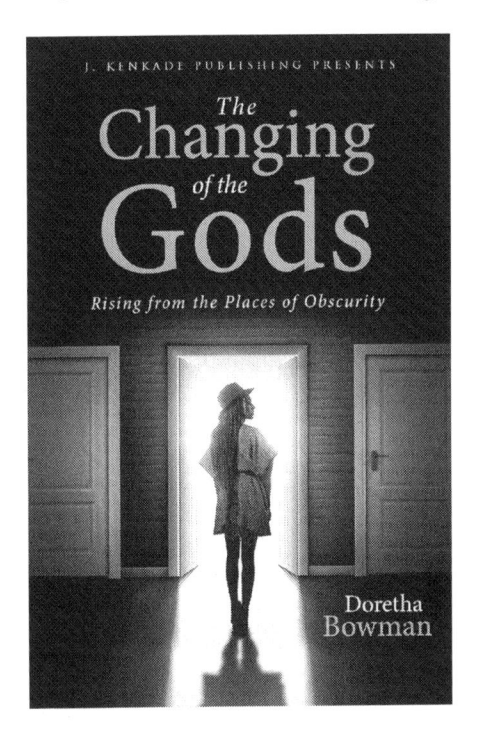

ISBN: 978-1-944486-26-6
Purchase at www.jkenkadepublishing.com

"The Changing of the Gods" describes one woman's life as it clung to the blind idolization of sin. From drug abuse, alcoholism, and victimization of sexual abuse, Doretha finds a way to make peace with her past through the aid of the guiding light of Christ, the true God. This book allows readers to acknowledge and rise from their places of obscurity to finally find the areas of their life that can be transformed by the light of Jesus Christ's salvation.

Also Available from J. Kenkade Publishing

J. KENKADE PUBLISHING PRESENTS

The Recipe
OF A GODLY
Woman

LaToya Geter-Shockley

ISBN: 978-1-944486-33-4
Purchase at www.jkenkadepublishing.com

A single pastor moves to a segregated town to lead a church deeply rooted in sin. Without knowledge of the sin, he begins to casually date the church clerk. While attempting to bring both sides of the town together, he meets a single mother filled with anger, betrayal, hurt and secrets and finds himself losing sight of God's direction for him. A life-threatening storm destroys the church and the town but opens his heart to the true woman of God.

Made in the USA
Columbia, SC
06 June 2019